9x5/04

Jeanne Modesitt

It's Hanukkah!

illustrated by Robin Spowart

Holiday House / New York

Text copyright © 1999 by Jeanne Modesitt
Illustrations copyright © 1999 by Robin Spowart
FIRST EDITION
ALL RIGHTS RESERVED
Printed in the United States of America
Design by Lynn Braswell

Library of Congress Cataloging-in-Publication Data
Modesitt, Jeanne.
It's Hanukkah!/by Jeanne Modesitt; illustrated by Robin Spowart.
p. cm.
Summary: A large mouse family joyfully celebrates Hanukkah.
Includes information on the history and some of the traditions of this holiday.
ISBN: 0-8234-1451-5
[1. Hanukkah—Fiction. 2. Mice—Fiction. 3. Stories in rhyme.]
I. Spowart, Robin, ill. II. Title
PZ8.3.M713It
[E]—dc21 1999 98-46704
CIP   AC

To the Light within us all

It's Hanukkah!

The candles are so bright,
they shine out into the night!

We gather round real close,
to the light we give a toast.

We listen to a tale;

our imaginations sail!

We all dance the horah,
even Great-Grandma Laura.

Mama gives us all treats,

lovely latkes to eat.

The dreidels, they are spinning,
and everyone is winning.

We give each other gifts;
our hearts, how they lift.

Aunt sings a happy song,

and everyone joins along.

We feel so much cheer;
we hug everyone near.

We at last go to bed,
after one more tale is read!

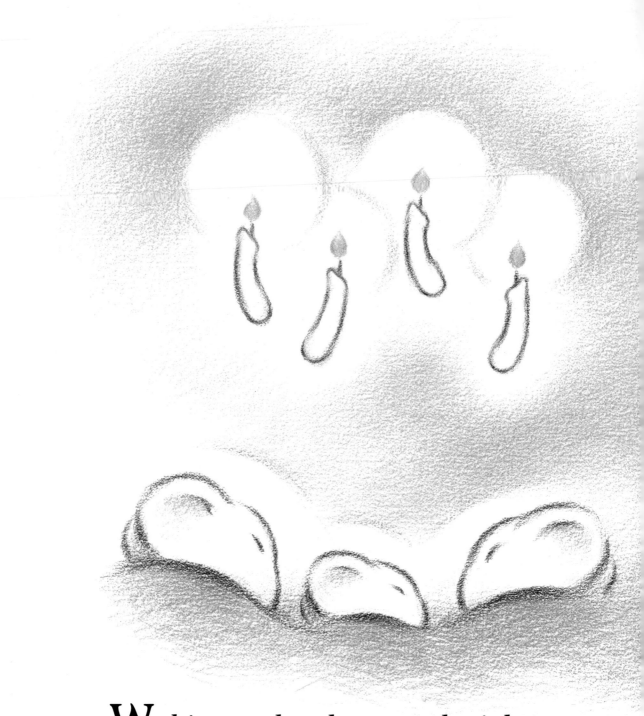

We kiss each other good-night,

and dream of dancing lights.

The Hanukkah Story

Over 2,000 years ago, Jews lived in the land of Judea, which is now called Israel. The center of their worship was the great Temple in the city of Jerusalem. In the Temple there was an eternal flame that burned day and night as a symbol of Jewish faith.

When the Syrian king Antiochus came to rule Judea as part of the Greek empire, he ordered Jews to give up their religion and follow the Greek religion instead. Some Jews obeyed the king, but many others did not. This made the king very angry. He sent his troops into Judea, where they burned down homes and killed many Jews. They tore up the inside of the Temple, destroying the precious eternal flame, then put up statues of Greek gods and goddesses.

In a small village called Modin, a man named Judah Maccabee led a small band of Jewish farmers, shepherds, and teachers in a fight against the king's army. This band, later to be known as the Maccabees, had no experience as soldiers, very few weapons, and was ten times smaller than the king's army. But they believed in what they were doing—fighting for the right to practice their religion—and this belief gave them strength, courage, and hope.

Finally, after three years of winning battle after battle against the king's army, the Maccabees reached Jerusalem and reconquered it. When they saw what the king's men had done to the Temple, they wept. But soon after, the Jews went to work: they scrubbed the Temple and threw out the Greek idols. The word Hanukkah means rededication. At last they were ready to rededicate the Temple to God.

But when they searched for oil to light the eternal flame, they found only one jug of sealed, pure oil—enough to last for just one day. But instead the oil burned on and on—for eight days! It was a miracle! With great joy, the Jews proclaimed, "Let us celebrate these days every year so that the story of the Maccabees' victory over the Syrian army, and the miracle of the oil, will never be forgotten!"

How the Mouse Family Lights Their Menorah

When the eight-day holiday of Hanukkah comes, the Mouse Family lights their Hanukkah candles. The candles are lit at sunset and are placed from right to left in a special Hanukkah menorah. Hanukkah menorahs have nine branches, to remind everyone of the little jar of oil that burned miraculously for eight days. The ninth branch is for the shamash, a helper candle that is used to light the other candles. On the first night, the shamash lights one candle, on the second, two, on the third, three—until the eighth night, when all candles are burning brightly. (The candles are lit left to right, so that the last candle added is the first lit.)

As the Mouse Family lights the candles, they say the Hanukkah blessings.

All three prayers are said on the first night, but on the remaining nights only the first two are recited.

1. Blessed art Thou, Adonai our God, Ruler of the Universe,
   Who has commanded us to kindle the Hanukkah lights.

2. Blessed art Thou, Adonai our God, Ruler of the Universe,
   Who has wrought miracles for our ancestors
   At this season in days of old.

3. Blessed art Thou, Adonai our God, Ruler of the Universe,
   Who has kept us in life and sustained us
   And enabled us to reach this season.

The Mouse Family's Favorite Latke Recipe
(Be sure to ask an adult to help.)

4 large peeled potatoes (3 pounds)
1 small onion
2 eggs
1/3 cup flour or matzoh meal
1 teaspoon salt
oil for frying

Grate potatoes and onion into a bowl. Drain off excess liquid. Add eggs, flour, and salt, and mix. Over medium heat, drop mixture by quarter cupfuls into a well-oiled, preheated frying pan. Fry on both sides until golden brown. Serve with applesauce, yogurt, or sour cream.

Makes 16 latkes.

How the Mouse Children Play
the Game of Dreidel

First, get two or more players together. Give each player the same number of objects. Nuts, raisins, pennies, or Hanukkah gelt will work. Hanukkah gelt are chocolate coins covered in gold foil. Next, everyone puts one object in the middle, which is called the pot. Now it's time to spin the dreidel! Each player takes a turn spinning.

If the dreidel lands on:

נ Nun: the player does nothing
ג Gimel: the player takes everything in the pot
ה Heh: the player takes half the pot (or half the pot plus one extra if there is an odd number in the pot)
ש Shin: the player puts one object in the pot

Whenever the pot is empty, or there is only one object left in it, each player puts one object in before the next spin. When one player has all the objects, he or she wins.
Then it's time to start all over again! Yippee!

O Hanukkah

O Hanukkah, O Hanukkah, come light the menorah.

Let's have a party, we'll all dance the hora. Gather 'round the

table; we'll give you a treat. Shiny tops to play with and

latkes to eat. And while we are playing, the

candles are burning low. One for each

night, they shed a sweet light, to remind us of days long a-

go.

mind us of days long a-go.

O Hanukkah, O Hanukkah, a festival of joy,
A holiday, a jolly day for every girl and boy,
Spin the whirling dreidel all week long.
Eat the sizzling latkes; sing the happy songs.
Now light them tonight then,
The flickering candles in a row.
(Retell the wondrous story of God in all His glory,
And dance by the candles' cheering glow.) REPEAT